MUSCLE CARS

Pre-Muscle Cars & GTOs

MUSCLE CARS

Pre-Muscle Cars & GTOs

MASON CREST

Nicholas Tomkins

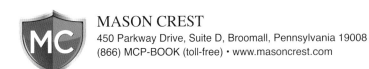

MASON CREST

450 Parkway Drive, Suite D, Broomall, Pennsylvania 19008
(866) MCP-BOOK (toll-free) • www.masoncrest.com

Printed in the United States of America

First printing
9 8 7 6 5 4 3 2 1

ISBN (hardback) 978-1-4222-4414-2
ISBN (series) 978-1-4222-4413-5
ISBN (ebook) 978-1-4222-7394-4

Cataloging-in-Publication Data on file with the Library of Congress

NATIONAL
HIGHLIGHTS

Developed and produced by National Highlights Inc.
Editor: Regency House Publishing Limited
Production: Becki Stewart
Interior and cover design: Regency House Publishing Limited
Text © 2020 Regency House Publishing Limited

CONTENTS

KEY ICONS TO LOOK OUT FOR:

Words to Understand: These words with their easy-to-understand definitions will increase the reader's understanding of the text while building vocabulary skills.

Sidebars: This boxed material within the main text allows readers to build knowledge, gain insights, explore possibilities, and broaden their perspectives by weaving together additional information to provide realistic and holistic perspectives.

Educational Videos: Readers can view videos by scanning our QR codes, providing them with additional educational content to supplement the text. Examples include news coverage, moments in history, speeches, iconic sports moments, and much more!

Text-Dependent Questions: These questions send the reader back to the text for more careful attention to the evidence presented there.

Research Projects: Readers are pointed toward areas of further inquiry connected to each chapter. Suggestions are provided for projects that encourage deeper research and analysis.

Series Glossary of Key Terms: This back-of-the-book glossary contains terminology used throughout this series. Words found here increase the reader's ability to read and comprehend higher-level books and articles in this field.

INTRODUCTION

What is a muscle car? First of all, let us eliminate what it is not: it is not a piece of Italian exotica, a Ferrari or a Lamborghini, cars, which are just too complex and too specialized; nor is it a German Porsche, which is too efficient and too clever by half; nor yet a classic British sports car, a Morgan, TVR, or Jaguar, which could never be regarded as fitting the bill. Sports cars, by and large, are not muscle cars, with two notable exceptions: the legendary AC Cobra of the 1960s, and the Dodge Viper of the 1990s. These followed the muscle car creed of back-to-basics raw power.

In effect, muscle cars always were, and always will be, a quintessentially North American phenomenon. The basic concept is something like this: take a mid-sized American sedan, nothing complex, upscale, or fancy, in fact, the sort of car one would use to collect the groceries in any American town on any day of the week; add the biggest, raunchiest V8 that it is possible to squeeze under the hood; and there it is.

Sports cars are not considered to be muscle cars. One exception is the AC Cobra, the English muscle car.

Dodge has been manufacturing muscle cars for years. This is a modern Dodge Viper.

The muscle car concept really is as simple as that. Moreover, the young men who desired these cars (and most of them were young and men) though that would change, were not interested in technical sophistication, nor handling finesse, nor even top speed. Cubic inches, horsepower, and acceleration rates were the only figures that counted. Muscle cars were loud, proud, and in your face, and did not pretend to be anything else. They might have been simple, even crude, but for roaring, pumping, tire-smoking standing starts, they were the business. To an American youth culture raised on drag racing, red-light street racing, and hot-rodding, they were irresistible.

The "Big Three" manufacturers soon woke to this fact and joined the power race to offer more cubic inches, more horsepower, and fewer seconds over the standing quarter. For a few short years, between 1965 and 1970, it seemed as though the race would never end. The result was often more power than the car (and the driver) could handle safely, but then part of the attraction was making a four-seater sedan go faster than it was ever intended.

But the situation could not last. The combination of high horsepower in the hands of young drivers saw accident rates soar, and insurance premiums followed suit. Moreover, the climate of the times was changing, with a whole raft of safety and emissions legislation coming into force in the late 1960s and early 1970s. So, even before the first oil crisis made itself felt, the first-generation muscle cars were already on their way out. By the 1980s, however, they were beginning to creep back, first with turbocharged fours, then V8s; by the 1990s, muscle cars were back with a vengeance: more "high-tech" than before, even sophisticated, with ABS, electronic fuel injection, and multi-valve engines. Manufacturers were by then talking virtuously about catalytic converters and air bags, but the truth was that performance was selling once again. Anti-social? Yes. Irresponsible? Of course. But one thing was certain, the muscle car was back.

The Chevrolet Impala was a prime candidate for a beef-up, having been downsized in 1961.

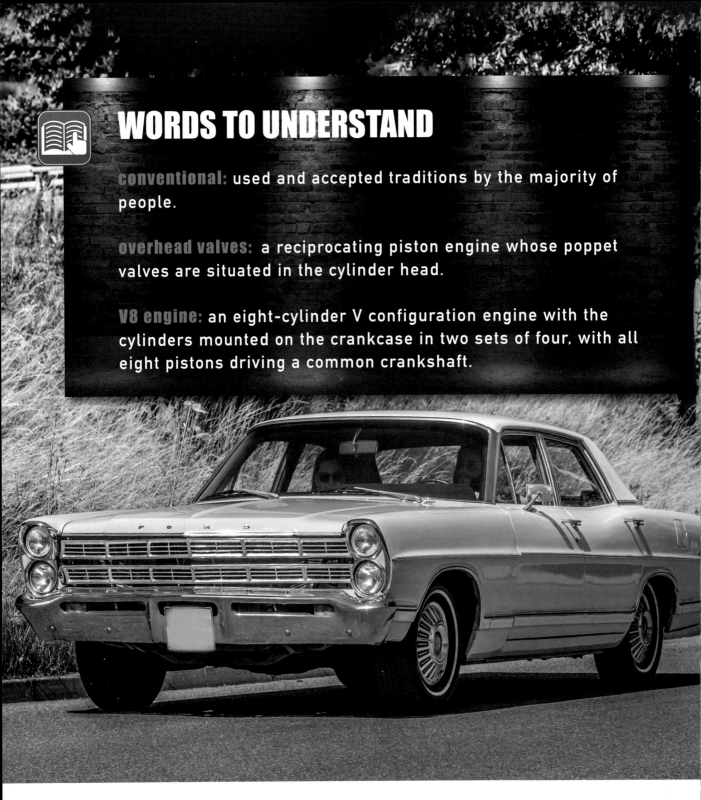

WORDS TO UNDERSTAND

conventional: used and accepted traditions by the majority of people.

overhead valves: a reciprocating piston engine whose poppet valves are situated in the cylinder head.

V8 engine: an eight-cylinder V configuration engine with the cylinders mounted on the crankcase in two sets of four, with all eight pistons driving a common crankshaft.

The Ford Galaxie is a big car but with a good deal of power.

CHAPTER 1
THE FORERUNNERS

Conventional wisdom has it that the Pontiac GTO was the first true muscle car. And it was, in the sense that it used a relatively large **V8 engine** crammed into an intermediate body shell, with performance the prime aim. But there had been plenty of high-performance V8s well before the GTO came along. They did not come into the same big engine/small car category, but performance was certainly part of their appeal. As to when such vehicles emerged from the primeval slime of automotive development, it is a case of how far back one is prepared to go.

Take the Ford flathead V8 of 1932. It may have been small, slow, and feeble by the standards of the 1960s, but for its time it also offered good performance at a low price. It formed the backbone of the U.S.A.'s early drag-racing

An ancestor of the muscle car, the Ford V8 Coupe.

OLDSMOBILE 88

Oldsmobile introduced the V8-engined 88 in 1949. Its design was hugely important as well as being one of the fastest automobiles in America in the early 1950s. The Oldsmobile 88 had a relatively small, light body and a large, powerful engine qualifying it for muscle car status. The car enjoyed great success, inspiring a popular 1950s slogan, *"Make a Date with a Rocket 88,"* and also the Ike Turner/Jackie Brenston hit record, *"Rocket 88,"* often considered the first rock and roll song. The Rocket 88 was so successful that it became the one to beat on the NASCAR (National Association for Stock Car Auto Racing) circuits. As a consequence, this led to increased sales on the forecourt. The 88 name remained in the Oldsmobile lineup until the late 1990s.

Scan here to take a closer look at the Oldsmobile 88.

movement, and a whole generation of hot-rodders grew up with it, coaxing ever higher speeds from Ford's first V8, which after all, is what defines a muscle car.

Then there was the Oldsmobile 88 of 17 years later. Once peace had been restored following World War II, most manufacturers made do with rehashes of early 1940s models, but the "Rocket V8" was the first of a new generation. The name alone indicated where Olds was heading: performance had by then become a key selling point, and the Rocket made an Oldsmobile the hottest American car of the early 1950s. With **overhead valves**, the Rocket could rev harder and faster than any flathead, and was so successful that Olds dropped its other engines and sold nothing but V8s until 1964.

Other manufacturers took note and swiftly introduced their own overhead-valve V8s, each attempting to outdo the other on sheer horsepower. Chevrolet's small-block motor, nicknamed "the hot one," was produced in a 265-cu in (4.34-liter) "Power Pack" version in 1955, with a four-barrel carburetor, dual exhaust, and 180hp (134 kW). That same year, Pontiac unveiled its own new V8, overhead-valve, of course, and in 1957 introduced the famous "Tri-Power" option: three two-barrel carburetors. Some Bonnevilles were given fuel injection in 1958 and the famous Super Duty parts began to appear the year after that.

Oldsmobile had no intention of being left behind and added a triple-carburetor set-up to the Rocket V8 in 1957, coaxing 300 hp (224 kW) from the 371-cu in (6.08-liter) J2 version. Chrysler had already beaten many of them to it with the 1951 "Firepower" V8, the first Hemi. Even with 180 hp (134 kW), its style was cramped by the heavy Saratoga into which Chrysler chose to fit it, but the Hemi's day would come. A foretaste of that appeared with the Dodge "Red Ram" Hemi in 1955, with 193 hp (144 kW) from 270 cu in (4.42 liters) and the D-500 (more cubes, more horsepower) in the following year. Ford, apart from offering supercharged Thunderbirds for a while, seemed somewhat left out, which is rather ironic when one remembers that it was Ford's original flathead that started the whole thing off. It was not until the energetic Lee Iacocca took over as general manager that Ford regained its performance image.

But Ford (and AMC) was the exception. A power race had already begun long before the muscle car boom of the mid/late 1960s. By 1964, when the GTO was unveiled, muscular V8s of over 400 cu in (6.55 liters) were commonplace. Perhaps we should take a look at some of these "pre-muscle" muscle cars.

An Oldsmobile 88 four-door sedan from 1954. Its V8 engine was a great success for Oldsmobile.

TEXT-DEPENDENT QUESTIONS

1. What automobile was considered to be the first muscle car?

2. What kind of engine did early muscle cars have?

3. What was the nickname of Chevrolet's 1955 muscle car?

Oldsmobile designed the 442 as a direct competitor to Pontiac's GTO.

RESEARCH PROJECT

Choose an early muscle car that you are interested in. Research how many were made, how many are left remaining, and how expensive they are to buy?

The GTO is considered to be the first true muscle car.

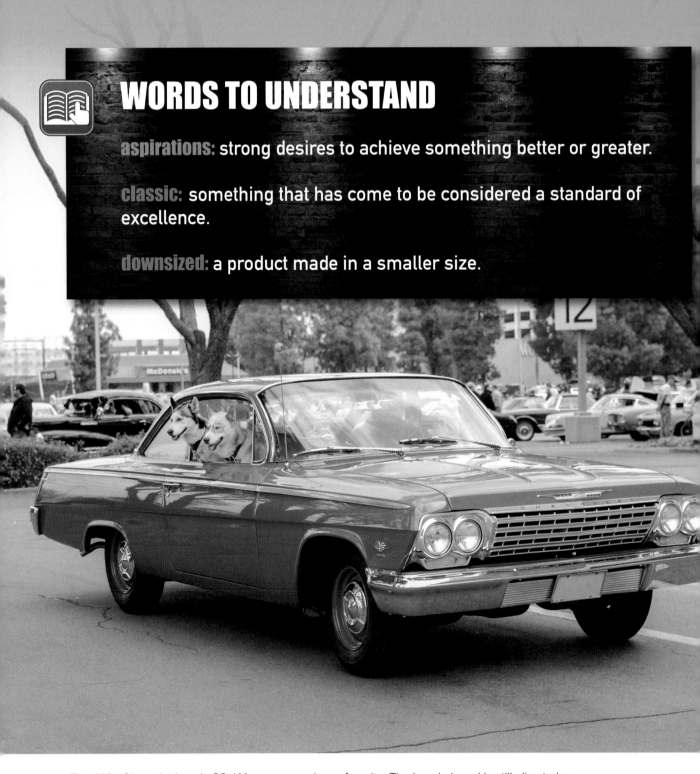

WORDS TO UNDERSTAND

aspirations: strong desires to achieve something better or greater.

classic: something that has come to be considered a standard of excellence.

downsized: a product made in a smaller size.

The 1961 Chevrolet Impala SS 409 was a muscle car favorite. The Impala brand is still alive today.

CHAPTER 2
GENERAL MOTORS

T ake Chevrolet's Impala, a prime candidate for a muscular beef-up, having been **downsized** in 1961; this was a case of less weight equalling more performance, particularly with a big V8 under the hood. The 1970s are usually remembered as the U.S.A.'s downsizing era, when cars became smaller and milder to suit an age of expensive gas. But the same thing had happened a decade and a half earlier, with big cars losing some of their surplus size and poundage, plus new U.S.-built compacts like the Ford Falcon and Chevrolet's own Nova appearing on the scene.

A Chevrolet Nova SS was downsized for more power and performance.

The 1961 downsized Impala was therefore a **classic** example, still available with large and decidedly meaty V8s, as long as one was prepared to lay down the extra dollars. There were two of them: the 348-cu in (5.7-liter) Turbo Thrust came in hot 340-hp or hotter 360-hp (single four-barrel or three two-barrel carburetors, respectively). If that was not quick enough, there was the legendary 409 Turbo-Fire, the V8 so revered by young drivers that the Beach Boys wrote a song about it. This came with 360-hp (268.4-kW) single four-barrel, 380-hp (283-kW) three two-barrel, or full 409-hp (305-kW) twin four-barrel versions, the most powerful of which would bump the price up by around $500. All had a high 11.25:1 compression, but a close-ratio four-speed transmission cost another $188. Even with the base 360-hp 409, the Impala two-door hardtop was convincingly quick, achieving 60 mph (96.5 km/h) in 7.8 seconds and turning in a quarter-mile time of 15.8 seconds. With the full-power 409, a Bel Air coupe made that 12.83 seconds; go for the aerodynamic bubble-top body in 1962, and it could hit an indicated 150 mph (241 km/h). By any standards, a 409-powered Chevrolet was fast.

A 1957 Chevrolet Bel Air. The Bel Air continued in various forms until U.S. production ceased in 1975.

16 Pre-Muscle Cars & GTOs

SUPER SPORT

Super Sport, or SS, is the iconic badge indicating the performance option package offered by Chevrolet on a limited number of its prestigious automobiles. All SS models come with distinctive "SS" markings on their exteriors and interiors. The first car to be honored with the SS package was the 1961 Impala. Other models bearing the SS badge include the Camaro, Chevelle, El Camino, Monte Carlo, Nova, and Chevrolet pickup truck. Today, SS models are produced by the GM Performance Division.

Scan here to take a look at the Chevrolet Nova SS 396.

If anyone remained unconvinced about the Impala's sporting **aspirations**, an SS package could be added by a local dealer. This could include power steering and brakes, heavy-duty springs and shocks, sintered metal brake linings, 8.00 x 14 whitewalls, a 7,000-rpm tachometer, and various "SS" badges. But maybe Impala buyers were not hot-car types, as only 456 of them ordered the SS package in 1961, and of those, a mere 142 paid extra for the 409. But that hardly matters, as in every other way the Impala 409 (especially with the flashy SS parts) qualifies as a pre-muscle muscle car. By 1962, the SS package had degenerated into a badges-only option, so one could look the part even with a basic six-cylinder Impala. But if one could afford it, the 409 was still there to give tire-smoking performance in the more conservative 1962 Impala.

If the downsized Impala represented an embryonic muscle car, then the compact Chevrolet II Nova took this idea to its logical conclusion. The Nova was Chevrolet's answer to home-built compacts like the Ford Falcon and Chrysler Valiant/Lancer, not to mention imported Volvos and Rovers. After the avant-garde Corvair, Chevrolet seemed determined to make its new compact as unthreatening as possible; and so it was, with a 90-hp (67-kW) four-cylinder base engine or 120-hp (89.5-kW) six. However, if one examined the options list hard enough, one would find that it was possible to have a choice of Corvette V8s installed by one's local dealer! The Nova had been designed to take both 283-cu in (4.6-liter) and 327-cu in (5.3-liter) V8s already, so no major surgery was involved. All the Nova V8s were the bigger motors, rated at 250, 300, 340, or 360 hp (186.5, 224, 253.5, or 26.5 kW).

It may look innocuous, but this 1966 Chevy II has the L79SS race package. It has all the serious upgrades.

That ultimate fuel-injected motor transformed the quiet, sensible Nova into a true muscle car, which could top 130 mph (209 km/h) and reach 60 mph (96.5 km/h) in a little over 7 seconds. To try to tame this performance, stiffer front springs were fitted to support the much heavier engine, with a front anti-roll bar, rear traction arms, and metallic brake linings. Almost everything else was standard, so a hard-driven Nova V8 would have been quite a handful, though a lot of fun.

It was not cheap though. The basic car cost just $2,200, and a dealer-fitted V8 could inflate that price by 50 percent, even before labor costs. But for lovers of subtlety, this was the one. There was nothing to indicate that the work had been done—no badges, special wheels, or wide tires. Only those who really knew their Novas would notice the dual exhaust tailpipes and 200-mph (322-km/h) speedometer. In fact, the whole option was distinctly low-key: a sporty SS package was offered in 1963, including bucket seats and extra chrome, but with no real performance aids. In the advertisement for the Chevrolet II Super Sports, Chevrolet didn't even mention the V8. Like the Nova itself, it seems they wanted to keep things quiet.

The same could not be said for the Corvette. America's only true two-seater sports car of the time, the Corvette is not always regarded as a muscle car: the classic muscle cars of the 1960s are all saloons or coupes. A Mustang might look like a sports car, but really it was a 2+2 coupe. Whether one includes the Corvette as part of the classic muscle car era or not, there is no denying that it was one of the fastest road cars one could buy in the early 1960s. In 1962, with

18 Pre-Muscle Cars & GTOs

Rochester fuel injection on the 327-cu in (5.3-liter) small-block V8, it had a better power-to-weight ratio than anything else, and could sprint to 60 mph (96.5 km/h) in less than 6 seconds. It also boasted 360 hp (268.5 kW), which was sky-high at the time.

Many Corvettes were raced, and the options list reflected that, with exotic items like an aluminum-cased transmission and large 24-gal (109-liter) fuel tank alongside the usual four-speed manual gearbox and sintered brake linings. There was all-new bodywork in 1963, for the Stingray Corvette, but the racing options were still there. Opt for the Z06 package, and one received the fuel-injected 327, a massive 36.5-gal (166-liter) tank, heavy-duty brakes, and suspension, plus knock-off wheels. That big tank enabled the Corvette to compete in endurance races, though only 60 cars were actually fitted with it. The stylish-looking cast aluminum wheels were a mixed blessing: they were porous and allowed air to leak out between rim and tire. Those heavy-duty brakes were interesting, too. Chevrolet had still not fitted new-fangled disks, making the drums as effective as possible instead: sintered metallic linings, power assistance, dual circuits, and Ram Air cooling. It sounded impressive, but the drum brake's sports car days were nearly over.

For 1964, there was cleaned-up styling and more power, though all Corvettes had the small-block 327: the big-block 396 did not appear until the following year. In base form, the 327 gave 250 hp (186.5 kW) at 4,400 rpm. Next up was the

The C1 was Chevrolet's first Corvette.

Chevrolet's Corvette was completely redesigned in 1963 to become the C2 Stingray.

300-hp (224-kW) L75 version, with Carter aluminum four-barrel carburetor. The 365-hp (272-kW) L76 added mechanical lifters, a hotter camshaft, and a Holley carburetor, plus an 11.0:1 compression. However, the ultimate Corvette still had fuel injection. Coded as L84 in Chevrolet-speak, the Ram-Jet injection motor produced 375 hp (279.5 kW) at 6,200 rpm and 350 lb ft (474.6Nm) at 4,400 rpm, enough for 0–100 mph (161 km/h) in 14.7 seconds and a top speed of 138 mph (222 km/h). A Corvette may not have been considered a "pure" muscle car, but it was certainly fast enough to qualify.

Meanwhile, another General Motors division was producing its own pre-muscle muscle cars. The Super Duty Pontiacs were, if truth be told, racing cars. Sure, they had seats, and lights, and a windshield wiper, and at a pinch they could be used on the road. But only if one were rich enough to buy one for personal use, and did not mind the stripped-out, lightweight interior. They remain a crucial part of muscle car history, however, paving the way for the GTO, the car that arguably started it all. The Super Dutys took Pontiac's staid image by the scruff of the neck, picked it up, and turned it around. By the time the GTO came along in 1964, the thought of a hot Pontiac was not only credible but desirable. Jim Wangers was a Pontiac promotions man who drag raced in his spare time. He and a group of keen young divisional engineers were instrumental in pushing the Super Duty options: after GM's racing ban in 1963, these same men turned to the next best thing, a hot Pontiac for the street. That was the GTO.

By their nature, the Super Duty Pontiacs were limited-production specials. Of all Pontiac models, Catalinas were the favorites, being the smallest and lightest of the full-sized Pontiacs. In 1962–63 these reached a nadir of development, before the GM racing ban called a halt. For 1961, they used the 389-cu in (6.3-liter) Super Duty, but the threat of Chevrolet's 409 led to the 421-cu in (6.9-liter) V8 in 1962. This became the ultimate Super Duty engine, strengthened with forged pistons and four-bolt main-bearing caps. It needed to be strong, as the unofficial power output was over 500 hp (373 kW), with twin Carter four-barrel carburetors. In the following year, a McKellar solid-lifter camshaft was added, with dual-valve springs, a transistorized ignition, and 12.5:1 or 13.0:1 compression: in top tune, that equated to 540–550 hp (402.5–410 kW).

To maximize the effect, Super Duty Pontiacs came radically lightened, with lightweight front ends and aluminum bumper brackets, trunk lids, and radiator supports. As an option, one could junk the standard windows in favor of dealer-fitted Plexiglas. Most radical of all were the "Swiss Cheese" Catalinas, with large holes drilled in their chassis. Weight was cut to just 3,325 lb (1508 kg), but they were considered too radical for Super Stock drag racing and were moved up to the new Factory Experimental class. Arnie Beswick drag raced one of these in 1963, managing a best quarter-mile of 11.91 seconds. Today, a Swiss Cheese with documented racing history would fetch over $100,000.

Of course, not all performance Catalinas were so exotic. By 1964, the 2+2 was being marketed as a sort of giant five-seat sports car "…as fine as you want—or as fierce." Top engine was a 370-hp (276-kW) version of the 421HO V8, which came with Tri-Power (three two-barrel carburetors) and 460 lb ft (623.8 Nm) at 3,800 rpm. It also weighed 4,000 lb (1814 kg), so the latest Catalina was no Super Duty, but with a quarter-mile time of 16.2 seconds it did qualify as a sort of muscle car, even if it was the boulevard type.

TEXT- DEPENDENT QUESTIONS

1. What muscle car did the Beach Boys write a song about?

2. What manufacturer made the Super Duty?

3. What does the Chevrolet SS badge stand for?

The very popular Stingray was Corvette's second-generation model.

RESEARCH PROJECT

Write a one-page essay explaining the differences in styling between automobiles manufactured in the 1950s and those made in the 1960s.

For its time the Corvette was very futuristic looking with unusual styling for the period.

WORDS TO UNDERSTAND

boy racer: a youth who likes driving very fast and aggressively in high-powered cars.

drag strip: a racetrack designed for conducting automobile and motorcycle acceleration events such as drag racing.

Hemi: an engine with a hemispherical combustion chamber, consisting of dome-shaped cylinders and piston tops.

Chrysler unveiled the C300 in 1955 with increased power to 300 hp (224 kW), hence the name.

CHAPTER 3
CHRYSLER CORPORATION

Chrysler's part in the muscle car story centers around the **Hemi**, that efficient, deep-breathing V8 that came to dominate the **drag strip** and NASCAR in the 1960s. But its origins lay much further back, in the 1951 Firepower V8. This motor's hemispherical combustion chambers allowed not only good breathing, but also a high compression plus plenty of space for big ports and valves. All well and good, except that the first 331-cu in (5.4-liter) Hemis were at a disadvantage, housed in heavy Saratoga saloons, and their performance failed to set new records.

This all changed in 1955, when Chrysler unveiled the C300. With power increased dramatically to 300 hp (224 kW), hence the name, this first of the famous "letter cars" set a new standard in performance. In fact, some people consider that this, not the Pontiac GTO, was the first true muscle car. Not that it was a stripped-down special. The letter cars were never **boy racer** specials, but luxurious two-door saloons—spacious, elegant, and well-appointed—but with blistering performance. Aimed at the top end of the market, Chrysler letter cars were expensive and exclusive, a fact reflected in a trickle of sales: in its best year, just over 3,600 were sold.

An early Chrysler V8 engine with a hemispherical combustion chamber.

Some of the gloss was lost in 1959 when the Hemi was dropped in favor of Chrysler's new wedge-head V8, but the loss was more than regained the following year, when the 413-cu in (6.7-liter) V8 was given Ram-Air induction for the 300-F. A hotter camshaft, low back-pressure exhaust, twin four-barrel carburetors, a more freely flowing air cleaner, and special distributor, and plugs helped push the power up to 375 hp (279.5 kW). That was with the standard 30-in (76.2-cm) long stacks, which gave tremendous mid-range torque: it peaked at 2,800 rpm, at which the torque was 495 lb ft (671.2 Nm). But performance suffered at higher revs, so just 15 cars were built with 15-in (38.1-cm) rams, an $800 option that also brought a four-speed manual gearbox, and 400 hp (298 kW). In truth, the 400-hp option was really intended for Daytona, but it paid off, with Greg Zigler setting up a Flying Mile record in a 300-F at 144.9 mph (233.2 km/h).

The Chrysler 300 set new records in terms of performance.

The same luxury-performance package continued as the 300-G in 1961, still with 375-hp long-ram and 400-hp short-ram options. Standard transmission was the Torquflite automatic, which in reality gave away nothing in acceleration to the three-speed manual (the four-speed had been dropped). Just to illustrate how luxurious the 300-G was, the options included air conditioning, remote control mirrors, a six-way power seat, and power door locks. An electric clock and front and rear center armrests were standard.

For 1962, there were four bucket seats in tan leather, with alternative colors on special order. By this time, the 300 (300-H now) had been downsized slightly, sharing parts with the cheaper Newport. The upsides were 300 lbs (136 kg) trimmed off the weight and acceleration as quick as the original Hemi 300s. If that was not enough, a

CHRYSLER 300

The Chrysler 300 "letter series" were high-performance luxury automobiles built by Chrysler from 1955 to 1965. The first year's model was named C-300, and the 1956 model was named 300B. Successive model years were given the next letter of the alphabet as a suffix (the letter "i" was omitted), The last year, 1965, was named the 300L, after which the model was dropped.

The 300 "letter series" cars were among the first high-performance cars to enter the American domestic market after World War II. Consequently, these cars along with other iconic cars of the time are now considered to be the muscle car's ancestors.

Scan here to watch this video about the Chrysler C300 series.

special engine option was announced in June. Overboring the 413 brought 226 cu in (6.9 liters) and a claimed 421 hp at 5,400 rpm on short-ram intakes.

Chrysler's downsizing did not last long, and for 1963 the 300-J was back up to full size, now with a 122-in (3.1-m) wheelbase and weighing over 4,400 lb (1996 kg). To compensate, the standard 413 V8 was squeezed up to 390 hp (291 kW) at 4,800 rpm, enough for a top speed of 142 mph (228.5 km/h). The return of a convertible option, and lower prices (though it was still not cheap at over $4,500 for the open-top) made the following year's 300-K sell just over 3,000 hardtops and 625 convertibles. These were hardly Mustang numbers, but this was the best-selling letter car of all. In its final year, the 300-L of 1965 had grown more flab, now up to 4,660 lb (2114 kg), and the 0–60 mph (0–96.5 km/h) time was now 8.8 seconds, a full second slower than the Hemi 300s. Still, it was mighty quick for such a big, heavy automobile, especially in 1965.

Remember that short-lived 426-cu in (6.98-liter) option for the 300? It lived on as the Max Wedge 426 in 1963, and thrived, as it fitted neatly into the new 427-cu in (7.0-liter) capacity limit for both NHRA Super Stock drag racing and NASCAR. In 1963, in "Stage II" form, it was very different from that offered as an option in the Chrysler 300-H. It was a pure racing engine, with three power options: the single four-barrel carburetor version produced 400 hp (298 kW) and was intended for stock car racing, which specified a single carburetor; twin four-barrels and an 11.0:1 compression allowed 415 hp (309.5 kW) at 5,600 rpm; finally, a 13.5:1 compression and twin carburetors brought 425 hp (317 kW). On paper, at least, this final development of the Max Wedge put out as much power as the second-generation Hemi that succeeded it.

The fins and chrome on the Chrysler 300 appeared in the late 1950s.

A C300L was the final mark from the "letter series" from 1965.

TEXT- DEPENDENT QUESTIONS

1. What is the origin of the Hemi engine?

2. How many Chrysler "letter" cars were sold?

3. What is a Max Wedge?

RESEARCH PROJECT

Write a one-page report about the invention of the Chrysler Hemi engine, its history, and its development.

A 1968 Chrysler 300 convertible is in the "non-letter series."

WORDS TO UNDERSTAND

boom: a widespread expansion of economic activity in a particular area.

corporate: relating to a corporation.

lip service: support for something that is expressed by someone in words but that is not backed up by deeds.

A 1950s Ford Fairlane. Models included a V6 and V8 version.

CHAPTER 4
FORD MOTOR COMPANY

Ford came late to the performance **boom** of the late 1950s: Chevrolet had its 409, and Chrysler its Hemi, but Ford's hottest was the 352-cu in (5.77-liter) 300-hp (224-kW) V8. That would have been impressive in 1955, but it was no longer so four years later. It is surprising, given Ford's commitment to "Total Performance" in the 1960s, and the string of successes in all forms of motor sport that followed. It really stemmed from the leadership of Robert McNamara, Ford's chief in the late 1950s, who saw cars as transportation rather than a source of excitement. That, and the company's strict adherence to the ban of the Automobile Manufacturers Association (AMA) on factory-sponsored racing. Chrysler and GM paid **lip service** to the ban but carried on helping private teams via the back door. But Ford followed it to the letter, and this was reflected in the cars it built for the road. Compare Ford's and GM's range of performance V8s in the late 1950s: there is no clearer illustration of the way in which racing stimulated the

A 1957 Ford Thunderbird convertible.

production of hot cars for the road. But from 1959, Ford's strict adherence to the rules began to relax. These things often come in cycles (remember that Ford had been first with a mass-production V8 in the 1930s), and in 1959 there were signs of a thaw, and of the realization that winning races really could help showroom sales.

The first sign came late in 1959, when a new 360-hp (268-kW) version of the 352-cu in (5.77-liter) motor was announced. Named "Thunderbird Super," "Interceptor," or "Super Interceptor," it was fitted with single Holley four-barrel, solid-valve lifters, 10.6:1 compression, and aluminum intake manifold. To cope with the extra power, the crank was of nodular cast iron. However, it was clearly not intended as an out-and-out muscle power unit: first Ford chose to fit it to the imposing heavyweight two-door, the Galaxie. The Galaxie was full-size in every sense of the word: for 1959, it measured almost 214-in (5.44-m) long and over 81-in (2.06-m) wide. Big, brash, and beefy, the Galaxie looked every inch the massive American cruiser that it was, though a new line in performance V8s was to give a further tweak to its image.

By 1961, however, the power race was getting into its stride, and failure to produce extra horsepower, even for a single season, would result in its being left behind. Ford had already served notice of its **corporate** change of heart during the previous year, informing the AMA that it was suspending its support of the ban on stock car racing. To

The Ford Galaxie was the competitor to the full-sized Chevrolet Impala.

ROBERT MCNAMARA

Robert McNamara played an important role in the American car industry. In addition to his role as a business executive, he served as the eighth United States Secretary of Defense from 1961 to 1968 under Presidents John F. Kennedy and Lyndon B. Johnson.

He joined the Ford Motor Company in 1946 at a time when the company was losing money. McNamara initially worked in the finance division of Ford. He quickly established strong accounting strategies that helped Ford to compete more successfully in the marketplace. Following his outstanding success, McNamara rose through the company ranks and was elected to director of Ford in 1957. In 1960, he was elected as president.

Scan here to take a look at the Ford Galaxie 500.

underline the fact, it took a Starliner Galaxie to Daytona and made 40 laps at an average 142 mph (228.5 km/h). Ford took 15 wins in Grand National races that year and announced it was also getting back into NHRA drag racing. There was no doubt about it, Ford was back in the performance business.

What did all this mean for ordinary drivers? The answer is simple: bigger engines, more power, and more speed. For 1961, a new 390-cu in (6.39-liter) version of the V8 was unveiled, with 4.05-in (102.9-mm) bore and 3.78-in (96-mm) stroke. Offered in the Galaxie Starliner, it came in three guises: 300-hp (224-kW) standard, 330-hp (246-kW) police variant, and 375-hp (280-kW) Thunderbird Super/Special, the last with a single four-barrel carburetor. Ford was now feverishly working to keep up with the multi-horse race, and in the middle of the year announced the Thunderbird Special 6V: 6V stood for "six venturi," thanks to three two-barrel carburetors, which helped produce 401 hp (299 kW). At first, the performance Fords came with a three-speed manual gearbox only, but now a four-speeder was optional. Better still, the Starliner was downsized slightly in the same year, so there was a little less weight to haul around. With a 6V under the bonnet, it could reach 60 mph (96.5 km/h) from rest in seven seconds, and run the quarter-mile in just over 15. At $425 extra for the 6V, most Starliner buyers, of whom there were almost 30,000 in 1961, opted for one of the smaller V8s or a straight six. There was no doubt about it: Ford had finally built a pre-muscle muscle car.

The Ford Thunderbolt was much lighter than the Galaxie, making it more competitive on the drag racing strip.

However, the company showed little sign of resting on any laurels, though the 390 had proved very competitive in drag racing. For 1962, its biggest V8 expanded again, this time to 406 cu in (6.65 liters). It shared some parts with the 401-hp 6V, and those extra cubes, plus the 6V's three carburetors, hot cam, and solid valve gear, which amounted to 405 hp (302 kW) at 5,800 rpm. On paper, this seemed something of an anticlimax, a lot of ballyhoo for a paltry 4-hp (3-kW) increase. But that would not be doing the 406 justice: it was actually a quite different engine from the 390. The block was all-new, with thicker cylinder walls. There were stronger pistons and connecting rods, while the transmission was substantially beefed up, too: a 9-in (22.86-cm) ring gear was used in the four-pinion differential, and there were 3-in (7.72-cm) drive shafts. The Borg-Warner four-speed transmission was a performance item, and both springs and shocks were stiffened up to cope with the extra speed at which Galaxie drivers were now likely to approach corners. Harder brake linings helped, too, and they were needed in a two-ton car that could top nearly 140 mph (225 km/h).

The 406 was not Ford's flagship for long, however, for it was announced late in 1962 and just six months later was topped by the 427. The 406 had not been in vain, however, for it was a stronger engine than the 390 and made a good basis for the still more powerful engines that Ford would be producing in the 1960s. However, it did give away a good 21 cu in (0.34 liters) to the NHRA/NASCAR 427.17-cu in (7-liter) capacity limit, which made the 406 look relatively puny against the 421 Pontiac and 426 Dodge.

So, 427 it had to be. There were two versions for the road: a single four-barrel carburetor motor with 410 hp (306 kW) and a conservatively rated 425-hp (317-kW) version with twin four barrels. Both were options on the big Galaxie and 500XL (the latter with sporting trim) for 1963, in two-door hardtop form. They cost $461.60 extra, but that did not stop nearly 5,000 big Ford buyers from signing the fatter check. So, they impressed on the street, but on the drag strip even radically lightened Galaxies, festooned with aluminum and fiberglass parts, were still too heavy for all-out drag-strip success.

That is why Ford turned to the lighter mid-sized Fairlane to spearhead its drag racing campaign, complete with the 427 V8. The Galaxie concentrated on NASCAR, where its newly aerodynamic fastback proved a real boon, and weight was not such a handicap.

The 427 never found its way into a road-going Fairlane: that was restricted to the drag race special Thunderbolt, of which Ford built about 100 for 1964. But road drivers could drive a hot Fairlane, too. It was not quite as muscular as the GTO, which was announced in that year, but still respectably fast. Its basis was Ford's 289-cu in (4.74-liter) V8, which was available in three rates of tune. In the mild "C" code form, with a 9.0:1 compression ratio, and lonely two-barrel carburetor, it produced 195 hp (145 kW); the "A" code 289 (9.8:1 compression, four-barrel carburetor) bumped that up to 225 hp (168 kW), which was warm but hardly hot; but the "K," or "Hi-Po" 289, with 10.5:1 compression, solid-lifter high-lift cam, and Holley four-barrel, made that 271 hp (202 kW). This was the same engine that powered the top-model Mustang in its first three years, but it worked equally well in the Fairlane.

As for Ford's luxury division, Lincoln Mercury, there were no real "pre-muscle" muscle cars, though for 1964 the division did announce the Comet Cyclone. This was a higher-performance version of the standard compact Comet, with Ford's 289 under the hood in 210-hp (157-kW) 9.0:1 compression guise. It was clearly not intended to out-gun the 271-hp Fairlane, and like most Mercuries it offered more luxurious trim than the Ford counterpart. It was not until 1966 that the Cyclone got serious. Now bigger, and sharing its body shell with the Fairlane, engine options included the 335-hp (250-kW) 390 in the new Cyclone GT. All the right parts were there, with a handling package, front disc brakes and four-speed manual gearbox all on the options list. The GT was truly Mercury's muscle car. But despite being handed the PR coup of running as pace car in the Indianapolis 500, sales were still disappointing, with fewer than 16,000 GTs sold that year: maybe Mercury drivers were not that bothered about performance.

TEXT- DEPENDENT QUESTIONS

1. What is the name of Ford's luxury division?

2. How long was the 1959 Galaxie?

3. What does AMA stand for?

This 1966 Ford Fairlane GT was starting to look more like a muscle car.

A 1969 Cyclone with a Cobra Jet engine was Mercury's muscle car.

RESEARCH PROJECT

Write a one-page essay on the interesting life of Ford boss Robert McNamara, and describe his many achievements in detail.

WORDS TO UNDERSTAND

acceleration: the process of speeding up.

supercharger: a device for increasing the fuel-air mix of an internal combustion engine in order to achieve greater efficiency.

versatile: having many applications or uses.

The Starlight coupe was a unique two-door body style offered by Studebaker from 1947 to 1952.

CHAPTER 5
STUDEBAKER CORPORATION

Studebaker? Pontiac built muscle cars, of course, as did Ford, Dodge, and Chevrolet—but Studebaker? Sometimes ignored for not being part of the "Big Three," little Studebaker did produce a couple of cars in the early 1960s that were indeed muscular, but being Studebaker it did so in a different way from everyone else, namely with supercharging.

The Avanti was a good basis for this, its exotic name reflecting long-hood coupe styling that was decidedly Italian in flavor. In some ways, it was quite advanced, the first full-sized American car with front disc brakes, which in this case were made by Bendix under license from Dunlop. Shorter than the average American sedan at 192 in (4.88 m), the Avanti was also much lighter at 3,400 lb (1542 kg). That was just as well, as Studebaker had access only to its own 289-cu in (4.74-liter) V8, while rival muscle cars were breaking the 400-cu in (6.55-liter) barrier. In its standard form the Studebaker unit produced 240 hp (179 kW), enough to make the Avanti R1 competitive with the milder V8 Mustangs but not enough to make it a muscle car.

But the R2 added a Paxton SN-60 **supercharger**, boosting power to 289 hp (215.5 kW) at 5,200 rpm (thus achieving the magic 1 hp per cu in) and 330 lb ft (447.5 Nm) at 3,600 rpm. As the R3, with a slightly enlarged 305-cu in (5.0-liter) unit, it made 335 hp (250 kW), though these were more expensive, and few were made. The R3 was actually hand-built at Paxton but only for serious and prosperous drivers.

Either way, both the R2 and R3 were fast. A four-speed R2 recorded 158.15 mph (254.51 km/h) over the measured mile in 1963, and apart from its exhaust, that car was almost stock. An R3 broke records with just over 168 mph (270 km/h) over the mile. *Road & Track* reckoned a time of 7.3 seconds for 0–60 mph (96.5 km/h) for the four-speed manual R2, and 8 seconds for the "power-shift" automatic.

Just as importantly, the Avanti handled well, unlike certain American-made muscle cars, and its standard disc brakes also functioned satisfactorily. "Here was an American car," wrote John Gunnell in *American Muscle Cars*, "that needed no apologies or alibis for either its acceleration or handling." Unfortunately, the American public failed to be impressed, and fewer than 4,000 Avantis of all types were built in 1963.

If the Avanti was Studebaker's last brave attempt to turn its ailing fortunes around at the eleventh hour with a radical new design, the Super Hawk was more conservative. It stemmed from the elegant Hawk coupe of 1951, designed by that stylists' stylist, Raymond Lowey, the man who transformed everything from tractors to toasters. Updated by Brooks Stevens in 1962, the Hawk was clearly inspired by contemporary Mercedes, and Studebaker certainly marketed the car as a grand tourer: in one publicity shot, a smartly dressed woman perches on a set of cases next to her Hawk, surrounded by travel posters, and no doubt pondering on where her GT might take her.

It may not have looked like any sort of muscle car (it was just too refined for that), but the Hawk could be made to perform like one when it was equipped with the Avanti R2's supercharged V8. Andy Granatelli (boss of Paxton Products, which supplied the R2's supercharger) drove a Hawk GT to just over 140 mph (225 km/h) over the mile at Bonneville early in 1963: buyers who wanted a car to the same specification merely had to tick the "Super Hawk" option box. That brought the R2 supercharged engine, power-assisted brakes, heavy-duty suspension with rear anti-roll bar, and traction bars, a twin-traction rear axle, 6.70-15 four-ply tires, and a tachometer.

According to *Motor Trend*, this added up to a quarter-mile time of 16.8 seconds and 0–60 mph in 8.5 seconds. They actually estimated the power at 300 hp (224 kW), though Studebaker itself never quoted figures for its top-

A 1956 Studebaker Silver Hawk came in four styles called Flight Hawk, Power Hawk, Sky Hawk, and Golden Hawk.

42 Pre-Muscle Cars & GTOs

A Studebaker Golden Hawk competing in the vintage racing car rally in Mille Miglia, Italy.

range V8, and claimed the supercharger delivered up to 4 lb (0.276 bar) of boost between 4,000 and 5,500 rpm. One interesting alternative to the standard four-speed manual transmission was the "Power-Shift" automatic, a Borg-Warner unit that was modified to suit the car. In position "1" and "2" it would not actually change up unless the driver did it manually, but in "D" it operated like a conventional automatic. And kickdown (an automatic down change at full **acceleration**) was available below 65 mph (105 km/h), with a manual down change possible up to 80 mph (129 km/h). The Avanti auto option was the same, reflecting the sporting bias of these cars.

Not all fast Studebakers of 1963–64 were supercharged, however. The R4 was yet another variation on the **versatile** little 289, ditching the Paxton blower in favor of twin four-barrel carburetors. It was not quite as powerful as the R2, with 280 hp (209 kW) but should have appealed to those who liked their muscle motors conventional. Studebaker chose the R4 for its Daytona, which was an updated restyled Lark, introduced in 1964. It seemed unassuming enough, but when R4-powered was capable of over 132 mph (212.5 km/h) and 0–60 mph in 7.8 seconds.

To put this into perspective, the Pontiac GTO, launched in the same year and hailed ever since as the first of the true muscle cars, was no faster to 60 mph (96 km/h) and 15 mph (24 km/h) slower on top speed. But then, as a hot car it looked the part, which the Daytona did not. Instead, Studebaker hoped to appeal to the man who favored subtlety. As well as the R4 (or any of the high-performance R V8s), it could be ordered with an Avanti suspension package: stiffer springs and shocks, anti-roll bars, and front disc brakes. So, it handled and stopped as well. The Daytona may not have looked like a muscle car, but it performed like one just the same, and far better than some.

The unusual Studebaker Avanti was heavily influenced by European cars.

TEXT- DEPENDENT QUESTIONS

1. Why was supercharging important for Studebaker?

2. Name three important Studebaker models.

3. What Studebaker model was inspired by Mercedes-Benz?

RESEARCH PROJECT

Write a one-page essay on the history of the Studebaker Corporation from when it was founded in the mid 1850s to its demise in the 1960s.

The Avanti combined safety and high-speed performance, it broke 29 records at the Bonneville Salt Flats.

WORDS TO UNDERSTAND

fanatics: people who are very enthusiastic about, and devoted to, an interest.

predecessor: a person who has previously held a position or job to which another has succeeded.

spartan: marked by austerity, frugality, or lack of luxury.

The car that started the muscle car revolution, the Pontiac GTO.

CHAPTER 6
PONTIAC GTO

The Pontiac GTO was the world's first true muscle car, which is the consensus opinion of just about everyone who has written on the subject. Of course, there were rumbling, grumbling, growling V8 sedans well before the GTO came along, but most were big, heavy, full-sized cars. The difference was that the GTO married one of those full-sized V8s with a lighter, intermediate body shell. The result was stunning performance in an affordable package, and the muscle car was born. Pontiac could actually have sold more than it built in 1964, and it was soon apparent that it was a new class of car. The odd thing was that it nearly didn't happen at all.

There was no long-term plan behind the GTO, no systematic market research or seven-year research-and-development program. The GTO came about because a few hot car **fanatics** were in the right place at the right time, when it could so easily have been the wrong time. In 1963, General Motors decreed that none of its divisions would go racing anymore or even produce overtly sporting cars. Pontiac was also restricted to a 300-cu in (4.92-liter) capacity ceiling on standard engines in intermediate cars. It was a bitter blow, as of all the General Motors marques Pontiac, like Chevrolet, prided itself on building performance cars. But in the GM pecking order, it did not have the resources of Chevrolet to develop an all-new car to get around this decision.

The 1966 GTO Tempest came with a standard four-cylinder engine.

It was even worse news for key Pontiac men like chief engineer John DeLorean, general manager Elliot "Pete" Estes and his **predecessor** Semon "Bunkie" Knudsen, engineers Russ Gee and Bill Collins, and advertising man Jim Wangers. All were hot car enthusiasts, convinced that the way to sell cars was by making image-building hot-rods. Fortunately for their fellow enthusiasts, all were in a position to do something about it.

Of course, Pontiac already made fast full-sized saloons, and Knudsen, Estes, and DeLorean in particular had transformed the division's image from staid to sporty in a few years. Super Duty engine-tuning parts were aimed at NASCAR racing and the drag strip, but super-stockers also rolled off the production line, road-legal and ready to go.

They were certainly fast, but also loud, bad-tempered, and decidedly **spartan** in comfort, while high-lift, long-duration solid-lifter cams, and multiple carburetors made them temperamental. In an effort to reduce weight, aluminum or fiberglass body panels were often fitted: Pontiac even drilled out the chassis of the Super Duty Catalina to trim further "fat" from the vehicle. These were specialized racing machines that took time to assemble, so they were not cheap. There was one other thing: a prospective buyer could not just stroll into his local Pontiac dealer and order one for the grocery run. In the words of author Thomas DeMauro, one had to have the right credentials: "Most

1967 saw the end of the first generation GTO.

The 1966 drag racing GTO was equipped with a Bobcat kit, which was a performance package.

required a National Hot Rod Association (NHRA) license, a letter of recommendation from God and compromising photos of the auto maker's general manager driving a Volkswagen to get one."

This was where the GTO broke new ground. It used a standard, smooth, reliable, and docile 389-cu in (6.375-liter) V8 straight out of Pontiac's parts inventory. But it was fast (and this was the master stroke) because it was shoehorned into an intermediate saloon, the Tempest, that weighed a whole 400 lb (181 kg) less than a full-sized car. So, it could do without rattly fiberglass panels, did not need the care and attention of a dedicated mechanic, and could afford to include all the hot car accessories like bucket seats and wide tires without upsetting the weight balance. Best of all, being a mix-and-match of existing parts that slotted neatly together on the production line, it was cheap. The GTO started at $2,700, which made for truly affordable performance.

This was the muscle car concept (a big V8 in a smaller saloon), and the GTO really did start it all. As it happened, the concept was easier for Pontiac to put into practice than anyone else, though it was more by accident than design. Fitting a big-block V8 into a smaller car was not as easy as it sounds, as the big-blocks from Ford and Chrysler, not to mention Pontiac's in-house rivals, were physically bigger than the small-blocks, so one could not merely take one out and slot the other in. All Pontiac V8s, on the other hand, from the 326 up to the big 421, were physically the same size, so it was

JOHN DELOREAN

John Zachary DeLorean was an American engineer famous for being the founder of the DeLorean Motor Company. He is also widely known for his great work and managerial contribution to General Motors. Throughout his long career in the automotive industry, DeLorean managed the development of a number of iconic vehicles including the Pontiac GTO, Pontiac Firebird, Pontiac Grand Prix, Chevrolet Cosworth Vega, and the DeLorean sports car. One of his greatest achievements was the running of the Pontiac Division between 1967 and 1968. In both of those years sales reached record levels. In 1969, he was asked to help turn around GM's troubled Chevrolet Division, which he did with ease.

In 1973, DeLorean left General Motors to start his own DeLorean Motor Company. However, production delays coupled with a depressed buying market was made worse by unexpectedly unfavorable reviews from public and the automotive press. Sadly, the car company that bore DeLorean's name went bankrupt in 1982.

Scan here to take a closer look at the GTO Tempest.

relatively simple to swap them around. That made a car like the GTO a relatively quick and easy variation to develop.

Better still, all those Pontiac V8s lost some weight in 1963. Without careful development, slotting a weighty big-block V8 into an intermediate car could result in a nose-heavy monster that would understeer at the slightest provocation. Pontiac's 389 was now light enough to minimize this problem. There was something else, too. The unit-construction Pontiac Tempest of 1963 was not up to handling the power and torque of the 389. But for 1964, it was redesigned with a conventional perimeter frame, four-link rear suspension, and solid rear axle, which could easily take a beefier output. Same-size engines, less weight, tougher chassis: it was almost as though the GTO was really meant to be.

Threading the Loops

But there was still one small problem: officially, no middleweight Pontiac could be offered with an engine larger than 300 cu in unless, of course, it was an option. So, when it was announced in October 1963, the GTO was not a model in its own right but a $295 option package that could be ordered with the LeMans Tempest in coupe, hardtop, or convertible forms. The clever thing was that the GTO option was not just a big engine, but a whole range of detail parts that made the GTO a model in its own right. It was sneaky, but it worked, getting around the 300-cu in ceiling and kicking off a legend all at once and the same time.

The name, incidentally, stood for Gran Turismo Omologato, which was another piece of marketing sleight of hand. It implied that Pontiac had applied to the FIA (Fédération Internationale de l'Automobile, the world governing body for motor sports) to have the car homologated for racing. That is why the legendary Ferrari GTO was so named. Some people were horrified that this parts-bin special should take on such a hallowed badge without earning the right. Others could not have cared less. Either way, the controversy simply created more publicity for Pontiac in general and the GTO in particular: like a celebrity publishing his warts-and-all autobiography, Pontiac could not lose.

Pontiac's Tempest lineup also included the GTO with a remodeling in 1965.

So what did one get for the $295? The basic engine was Pontiac's existing 389-cu in (6.375-liter) V8, which in standard tune produced 325 hp (242 kW) at 4,800 rpm. The engine was not totally "off the shelf," however: the standard heads were replaced with 421 HO items, with big valves, and allowing a 10.75:1 compression with the flat-top pistons, and other changes included heavy-duty valve springs and a Carter four-barrel carburetor, plus different lifters and camshaft. If 325 hp was not enough, one could change the option and specify Tri-Power, three Rochester two-barrel carburetors in place of the single four-barrel, which produced 348 hp (259.5 kW) at 4,900 rpm. The triple carburetor set-up was a hangover from Pontiac's Super Duty days. Either way, one achieved eye-popping performance.

In January 1964, *Motor Trend* tested a GTO, a four-speed convertible that rocketed to 60 mph in 7.7 seconds and covered the standing quarter-mile in 15.8 seconds. Meanwhile, *Car and Driver* published a now-famous test between the GTO and a genuine Ferrari GTO. It was a nice idea, except that in its eagerness to out-GTO the Ferrari, Pontiac supplied two test cars, both fitted with tuned 421-cu in (6.9-liter) engines that managed 0–100 mph

The 1965 model year Pontiac GTO had a slightly longer body, but with the same wheel base as the 1964 model.

(161km/h) in 11 seconds (which *C&D* headlined on its front cover) and turned in a standing quarter of 13.1 seconds. It really made a nonsense of the whole point of road-testing cars: no one could walk into his Pontiac dealer and order a GTO like that. On the other hand, it worked for Pontiac. *Car and Driver* declared that in many ways the U.S.-built GTO was better than the Italian vehicle. This delighted and infuriated so many enthusiasts that the magazine was still getting mail on the subject two years later.

However, in the real world, it was not just a case of choosing between two states of tune: the GTO buyer could specify any of a bewildering array of other options, covering interior, exterior, and mechanics. It was fun, it helped to "personalize" the car, gave dealers and manufacturer extra profit mark-ups, and was always part of the muscle car buying experience. The basic transmission was a three-speed manual, with floor-mounted Muncie shift. Or one could have a wide-ratio or close-ratio four-speed, with at least half a dozen different rear axle ratios. There was an automatic, too, a two-speed Super Turbine, which was upgraded for the GTO with a high-output governor to allow higher speed and rpm up-changes, as well as higher clutch capacity, among other things. These detail changes to

GTO also saw several mechanical changes in 1967. The Tri-Power carburetion system was replaced with a single four-barrel Rochester Quadrajet carburetor.

existing parts indicated that the GTO was not a hurried-through option, but well thought out and developed, notwithstanding what was written earlier in this book.

Suspension changes were limited to high-rate springs, specially valved shock absorbers, and longer rear stabilizers than standard, backed up by wider 6-in (15.2-cm) rim steel wheels and low-profile red-stripe tires. Not everything changed, though, and the 325-hp GTO carried the same 9.5-in (24.1-cm) drum brakes as the six-cylinder Tempest; this would be a GTO weak spot for quite a while. The only concession to the GTO's 115-mph (185-km/h) top speed was the option of semi-metallic linings, said to reduce fade.

There was no chance of anyone mistaking the GTO for a pedestrian Tempest or LeMans, or for that matter an Oldsmobile Cutlass or F85, Buick Skylark, or Chevrolet Chevelle/Malibu, all of which used the same A-body platform. As well as those wider red-stripe tires, there were two fake hood scoops with chrome-ribbed trim and GTO badges on the grille, rear end, and flanks. Inside, bucket seats were standard, with an engine-turned trim on the dashboard. What one did not get was full instrumentation, and the standard set simply comprised a speedometer and fuel gauge, backed by various idiot lights. Keen drivers could specify extras, such as a semi-circular tachometer, which indicated an optimistic maximum 7,000 rpm. It also proved to be wildly inaccurate and was prone to emit a steady hum, later fixed: it is now a collector's item.

So, what did the buyers think of Pontiac's latest option pack, the GTO? They loved it. Despite being on sale for only part of the 1964 season, over 7,000 coupes, 6,600 convertibles, and over 18,000 hardtops were sold as GTOs, which was not bad for what was really just another option.

If there had been any annoyance among General Motors top brass at Pontiac's bare-faced audacity with the GTO, it did not show. Anything the senior management may have felt was mollified by the 75,000-plus GTOs that were sold in 1965. In any case, the gates were open now, and in its second year the GTO faced in-house GM competition from the Oldsmobile 4-4-2, Buick Gran Sport, and Chevrolet Malibu SS.

But one has a head start, being first, and the GTO's first-year impact paid off in its second year. Pontiac made the most of that more aggressive front-end styling, with vertical twin headlamps and one large hood scoop in place of the two smaller ones. Bolder front grilles and concealed taillights completed the exterior changes, while inside there was a new Rally gauge option, which brought a proper full-sized tachometer as well as water temperature and oil pressure gauges. The brakes remained unchanged except for optional aluminum-finned drums, more efficient at dissipating heat and so reducing fade. The optional wire wheel covers now had slots to allow cooling air in, but the real solution was to ditch the drums altogether in favor of power-assisted discs.

The big news was more power, a clear indication that the Pontiac performance restriction had been swept away by the GTO's success. Both four-barrel and Tri-Power V8s received better breathing from altered cylinder heads and inlet manifolds. That boosted the base engine to 335 hp (250 kW), enough for a 16.1-second quarter-mile, and 0–60mph in 7.2 seconds. The triple-carburetor Tri-Power was fitted with a new camshaft as well, with 288/302 degrees duration, to

This GTO hardtop has found its way to Russia.

produce 360 hp (268 kW) at 5,200 rpm. To promote its new star, Pontiac emphasized the big cat theme. "Have new tigers," went one, "need tamer. Apply at any Pontiac dealer." There was also the "GeeTO Tiger" record, revealing the sounds of a GTO being driven hard at the GM Proving Ground in Milford, Michigan. That costs 50 cents, but if pocket money did not stretch quite that far, 25 cents bought a set of giant color photographs of GeeTO Tiger in action.

The year 1968 was a high point for the GTO, the year when it finally became a model in its own right, not simply an option package. Better still, sales were up 28 percent on the previous year, with nearly 100,000 cars sold. As ever, the hardtop was by far the most popular, making up 75 percent of those 100,000 vehicles. A substantial minority (just over 10,000) went for the coupe, and nearly 13,000 GTO buyers opted for convertibles. But they were not all performance freaks: fewer than one in five paid extra for the 360-hp Tri-Tri-Power set-up.

Whatever the model mix, the GTO was the undisputed king of the muscle cars in 1966, selling more than anyone else, if one ignores the pony cars. It was quite an achievement, as the marketplace was now crowded with a host of rivals trying to muscle in on the quick-car scene. Ford fitted a 390-cu in (6.394-liter) V8 to the Fairlane GT and GTA, while Mercury did the same, turning the Comet into the Cyclone. More seriously, both could be had with a 427-cu in (7.0-liter) option, and Chrysler's 426-cu in (6.98-liter) Hemi was just coming on stream. GM cars were at a decided disadvantage, as the parent decreed that no GM intermediate car could be sold with an engine bigger than 400 cu in (6.55 liters), though Buick got a 401-cu in (6.57-liter) dispensation. This time, they would make it stick: there would be no sneaky big-engine options to get around it.

However, this did not appear to harm GTO sales, which were aided no doubt by the new Coke-bottle styling of that year. This little kick-up over the rear wheels, so ubiquitous in the late 1960s and early 1970s in cars built all over the world, rather than just in the U.S.A., had originated in Pontiac's full-sized cars of 1963. The hardtop got a semi-fastback, which combined rakish rear pillars with a more upright rear window. It looked good but created a serious blind spot. Other changes were minor, though did include a Ram Air option for the Tri-Power engine. As well as the foam-sealed air pan, it included a longer-duration camshaft (301/313 degrees) and heavy-duty valve springs. Strangely, it was quoted at the same 360 hp as the standard Tri-Power. Either way, this was the final year for the complex three-carburetor set-up.

But did the GTO deserve its best-seller status? Was the original muscle car still the best? In April, *Car and Driver* pitted the Pontiac against its five main rivals and was ambivalent about the result. "Certainly the sportiest looking and feeling car of the six," went the write-up, "Its shape, its paint, its flavor, say GO!… but it was its suspension that let it down." It suffered severe axle tramp, "bordering on the uncontrollable," and only the Comet was worse. The test driver for track sessions at Bridgehampton (racing driver Masten Gregory) was unimpressed by the GTO's cornering power as well: "The suspension is certainly too soft … it tends to float and bounce in the corners."

It might still have won out as a comfortable boulevard cruiser with a strong image, except that the test car came with the Royal Bobcat tuning package. An option offered by a Michigan Pontiac dealer, this consisted of richer jets, thinner head gaskets, positive locking nuts, and retuned a distributor. These were not huge changes, but they made the GTO the most powerful car of the six, despite having the smallest engine. The trouble was, it turned the quiet, docile 389 into a recalcitrant beast. Hard to start and reluctant to keep going when cold, it idled noisily at 1,000 rpm and guzzled gas at 11 mpg (5.5 km/liter) even at steady speeds. To add insult to injury, the fuel pump drive sheered off during the test, the 389 shed its fan belt on the drag strip, and the left upper control arm of the rear suspension broke. Twice the GTO had to be sent back for repairs before the test could continue. "When [the GTO] was first produced," concluded *Car and Driver*, "we tended to forgive some of its handling foibles because of its newness and exciting originality, but now, in the face of sophisticated packages like the 4-4-2, it needs improvement."

The stacked headlights of the 1960 GTO were a distinctive feature of Pontiacs of the time.

A Change of Climate

One generally associates the early 1970s with a downturn for muscle cars, when emission and safety standards were beginning to bite. But the climate had been changing from a time years earlier. California-bound GTOs had been fitted with closed crankcase ventilation since early in 1964, and with air injection from 1966. For 1967, the "GeeTO Tiger" was dropped, and even John DeLorean emphasized safety in his public statements.

As for the GTO, it acquired a whole range of new safety features: dual-circuit brakes with those long-overdue and badly needed discs (still only an option though), soft window handles, and coat hooks, a breakaway mirror, and a collapsible steering column. Just a few years' worth of muscular tire-smoking antics, with the emphasis firmly on performance, had been enough to have safety campaigners up in arms. If one considered the number of people killed on U.S. roads each year, the critics had a point, especially while manufacturers paid so little attention to safety. So, maybe it is possible to liken the 1960s muscle car era to a teenage party: it was not yet over, but responsible parents were standing around outside the house, complaining about the noise and bad behavior, and it would not be long before one of them marched in and pulled the plug out of the stereo.

1967 saw the last of the first generation GTOs.

It was all change for the GTO in 1968 with the second generation redesign.

So, Pontiac soft-pedalled its advertising for 1967, which merely disguised the fact that alongside the new safety features was a bigger engine. With a new block, the 389 was bored out to a full 400 cu in (6.55 liters) to take advantage of the GM capacity limit for intermediates. There was actually an economy version of this engine, with low 8.6:1 compression and two-barrel carburetor, rated at 255 hp (190 kW), and this came with an automatic transmission only; fewer than 4 percent of GTO buyers actually chose it. One suspects it was a concession to the safety campaigners. Most buyers went for the standard four-barrel 400, for which Pontiac claimed the same 335 hp as the old 389. In place of the Tri-Power, there was a 400HO (High Output) version with 288/302 cam, free-flowing exhaust manifolds and a claimed 360 hp, again exactly the same as its predecessor. The ultimate GTO power unit for 1967 was the Ram Air, which used a working air scoop to funnel cold, dense air straight into the intake at speed. As part of the package, it came with a peakier camshaft (301/313 timing) and low rear axle ratio of 4.33:1. That made it a mite buzzy on the highway, and the tuned Ram Air could get hot and bothered in warm weather.

Despite all the extra equipment, this engine put out the same 360 hp as the HO, if one believed Pontiac. But really, this was a sign of the times: manufacturers were understating power outputs to avoid drawing flak from the safety campaigners. Maybe they went too far, for only a small minority of GTO buyers paid extra for Ram Air in 1967. The actual figure was fewer than one in a hundred.

The styling of the 1969 GTO was markedly different from its first-generation predecessor.

In the new climate, Pontiac would have preferred, in any case, to concentrate on the new disc brake option, which brought vented power-assisted front discs with four-piston callipers. There were separate circuits for the front and rear, so there were still brakes if one of the circuits were to fail. A three-speed automatic, the TH-400, was another new option, finally replacing the aging two-speed. More noticeable was the extra-cost hood-mounted tachometer. It was a neat and novel idea, though in practice it tended to mist up in damp weather and was difficult to read at night, while its delicate components did not cope well with full-blooded hood slams.

As with most muscle cars, options were part of the fun. The GTO buyer faced lists and lists of options: quite apart from the three body styles, 12 different engine/transmission combinations, and ten rear-axle ratios, there were the endless detail touches available either on the production line, or dealer-fitted. The dealer could, for example, fit an engine block heater, ski rack, or litter basket (the last in red, blue, black, or beige). Factory options were extremely involved, with everything from the Ram Air engine to heavy-duty electrics or a reading lamp. If there seemed to be too much choice (there were nearly 100 individual factory-fitted options alone), there were various option groups. For the production planners, parts men, and dealers, it must have been a nightmare.

GTO sales fell in 1967, from that all-time high, to 81,722 vehicles. What with the new pro-safety climate and a horde of bigger, more powerful competitors, one might have forgiven Pontiac for expecting worse in 1968. But the GTO bounced back. With new more rounded styling and more power, sales crept back up to over 87,000, and the GTO was even voted Car of the Year by *Motor Trend*. (The new shape had much to do with this fresh lease on life.) Now in hardtop and convertible forms only, the GTO was more sporting than before, the classic long-hood/short trunk shape on a shorter 112-in (2.84-m) wheelbase. This was shared with the Tempest, but the GTO added trimmings like out-of-sight wipers and dual-exhaust tailpipes. More obvious was the chrome-free Endura rubber bumper. Made from high-density urethane-elastomer, it would resist denting and even bounce back into shape after minor knocks. However, the standard chrome version was also available. The concealed headlamps were a new option, echoing the 1967 Camaro, and revealed by slide-away vacuum-operated doors in the grille. That was fine, until a leak developed in the actuator, and "winking" GTOs (one headlamp door closed and the other open) were often seen as the cars aged.

There was an all-new interior as well, with lots of wood grain trim and a new three-pod instrument panel, though on this supposedly sporting car one still had to pay extra for a tachometer. Despite new moves to clean up emissions (redesigned combustion chambers and changed ignition timing) the 400-cu in (6.55-liter) V8 offered more power, with 350 hp (261 kW) in standard four-barrel form or 265 hp (197.5 kW) in two-barrel form. Meanwhile, a new Ram Air II system featured cylinder heads with bigger intake ports and freer-flowing exhaust ports, a cam with hotter timing and higher lift, plus bigger valves. Power was up, but only slightly, to 366 hp (273 kW), while the non-Ram Air 400HO remained at 360 hp. There was just one drawback to Ram Air: it could not be used in the rain, as the open hood scoops let water in. So, it came as a package in the trunk of the car; at the first sign of rain, the driver had to stop and swap back to blanked-off scoops. It is hardly surprising that Pontiac did not sell many.

The big news for 1969 was The Judge. Pontiac had long been pondering the fact that the GTO range fell short of both a budget muscle car and a premium model, during a period in which the competition offered both. There was a whole range of budget performers, such as Pontiac's own 350 HO-powered Tempest, which were cheaper than any GTO and cost less to insure, an important factor for younger drivers. But it was never promoted by Pontiac as a muscle car, and sales reflected that fact. So, company engineers put a proposal together for a hopped-up Tempest to fill the gap and sent it up to John DeLorean. He rejected it and ordered that the car be upgraded as a new range-topper for the GTO instead. This was The Judge.

It was, if truth be told, little more than an existing GTO with Ram Air and loud colors. Pop art was influencing car design in the U.S.A., and bright colors with suitable decals were becoming part of the muscle car look. Sure enough, the first 2,000 Judges were finished in Carousel Red, with extrovert 60-in (1.52-m) rear spoiler, bubble-letter "The Judge" logos, and stripes. Mechanically, the Judge used the 1968 400HO power unit, but with Ram Air

The Judge was a GTO with bright paint and eye-catching graphics. Mechanically, it used the 400HO with Ram Air, plus heavy duty suspension, and wide, low-profile tires.

III, heavy duty suspension, Rally II wheels, and G70 x 14 tires. For an extra $332 over the price of the standard GTO, it offered a real eyeful, and came in both hardtop and convertible forms, though only 108 of the latter were built, compared with nearly 7,000 hardtops.

There were few other major changes for the GTO that year, though the latest Ram Air IV system now claimed 370 hp (276 kW) at 5,500 rpm as a result of improved intake ports and limited-travel hydraulic lifters, plus a slightly higher lift on the cam. Both this and Ram Air III, incidentally, were now driver-controlled. If it rained, the driver no longer had to stop, get out, find those closed-off hood scoops, and fit them. Now, the driver simply pulled a knob, and the scoops closed themselves.

Seventies Slide

It was just as well that Pontiac had The Judge for 1969, and sold nearly 7,000 of them, for GTO sales slid to a little over 72,000 that year. That was a drop of almost 20 percent and heralded the rapid slump in GTO sales during the early 1970s. In 1970, they fell by nearly half, to 40,000, and to just over 10,000 in 1971, when the GTO was outsold ten to one by its bread-and-butter stable mate, the Tempest. Its fall from grace was sudden and dramatic, and its end was near. In a way, the GTO's tough performance image was biting back: along with other muscle cars in the early 1970s, it was suffering from spiralling insurance costs, especially for young drivers, as experience revealed that cheap tire-smoking muscle cars and the under-25s were not always a good mix.

However, if the 1970 GTOs were anything to go by, it was simply business as usual. There had been complaints that the 1968 body shell left the GTO looking a little too refined and effete. So, the 1970 version was given bigger

The 1969, GTO including The Judge was upgraded to include the Ram Air III engine.

wheel-arch moldings and a new aggressive front end with quad headlamps. There was a similar theme under the hood. GM had belatedly lifted its 400-cu in capacity limit, and Pontiac responded with a 455-cu in (7.46-liter) V8. However, this was not the high-horsepower option. Instead, the 455 was a relaxed, torquey engine in a mild state of tune, aiming to provide a suitable boulevard power unit for luxury GTOs: that was underlined by 360 hp (268.5 kW) but over 500 lb ft (678 Nm) of torque. Otherwise, the familiar 400s continued, offering from 350 hp (260 kW) in the standard four-barrel to 370 hp (276 kW) with Ram Air IV.

Incredibly, for 1970, 9.5-in (24.1-cm) drum brakes around, with no power assistance, were still the standard brake set-up, though handling was at last improved with a rear anti-roll bar and a larger front bar. Spring rates were unchanged, but the suspension mountings were beefed up, and a new variable-ratio power steering system was offered. The result was a great improvement, and the GTO finally had handling to match its straight-line performance. The Judge was still part of the line-up ("After a few moments of respectful silence," went the 1970 advertisement, "you may turn the page"), and there was a new GTO-related budget muscle car, the GT37, based on a Tempest two-door. And there was an unusual new option that year. The Vacuum Operated Exhaust

The Judge originally only came in carousel red, but later, other colors became available.

The sporty red leather interior of The Judge.

(VOE) allowed the driver to move the exhaust baffles via a dashboard switch, giving more noise and horsepower at the pull of a dashboard knob. It was not quite as anti-social as it sounds, with the choice between a fully legal standard GTO exhaust and the quiet LeMans equivalent. Only 223 GTO buyers specified the VOE.

By 1971, Pontiac seemed to have given up on the GTO. It was changed very little, apart from a bigger grille and hood scoops, and there was no advertising in the mainstream magazines at all. Compression ratios were dropped to allow all GTOs to run on regular fuel, and a new round-port version of the 455 HO was listed at just 335 hp (250 kW). It was clear that Pontiac had better things on its mind than promoting the aging GTO: the Trans Am was now its performance flagship, while the Firebird had been redesigned for 1971. Ram Air III and IV were dropped. Power started at 300 hp for the standard 400 (now with an 8.2:1 compression), with the 335-hp 455 the hottest GTO one could buy, though the car looked as macho as ever.

Only 10,532 GTOs found buyers in 1971, and for 1972 Pontiac did the obvious thing and relegated it to option status: the GTO was now an option pack on the LeMans, though that did make it cheaper. Of course, this was exactly how the GTO had started, as a low-key option on a bread-and-butter model in 1964, which now seemed a lifetime away. Unless one were a GTO enthusiast, there seemed little point in buying one, as a LeMans could be

A 1970 GTO Judge.

specified at the same level of performance with a different range of options. Not surprisingly, GTO sales slumped again, to just 5,807 in that year. Of course, all muscle cars were suffering in the early 1970s, but the GTO lost out more than most. There were very few changes to the car, though what looked like a drastic power cut was due to a change to net rather than gross power measurement. The base 400 now started at 250 hp (186 kW), with 300 hp (224 kW) from the 455 HO.

The year 1973, according to author Thomas DeMauro, was a lost opportunity for the GTO. Those 20-something baby boomers who had bought the original were now approaching comfortable middle age: they wanted more comfort and prestige, maybe even four doors, and DeMauro reckons Pontiac had just the GTO for them. Instead, it was unveiled in 1973 as the Grand Am, which sold well. According to DeMauro, Pontiac wanted the GTO to return to its roots as a proper high-performance muscle car.

In 1970, hidden headlamps were deleted in favor of four exposed round ones.

In the 1970s, Pontiac launched the GTO in a variety of colors such as this one in bright yellow.

So, the 1973 model was based on the latest LeMans coupe with the controversial Colonnade styling. Not everyone liked it: the single front headlamps and heavy chrome bumper seemed like retrograde steps, and it was certainly lacking the sheer threatening presence of the 1971 and 1972 GTOs. Early literature indicated that the car would be available with a 310-hp (231-kW) Super Duty 455, but when production started that was reserved for the Formula and Trans Am. Once again, the GTO option was not advertised, and even Pontiac's 1973 new model announcement contained just one, very small, reference to it. Only 4,806 people chose to add the GTO option to their LeMans in 1973, the worst sales figure ever.

By rights, the GTO should have died then and there, but at the eleventh hour, Pontiac decided to give it another chance. This time they really did go back to the GTO's roots, reverting to the compact Ventura. Now this was promising. The Ventura may have been an economy car, almost identical to other X-body GM siblings like the Chevrolet Nova, but it was up to 800 pounds (363 kg) lighter than the LeMans. Even with a smaller engine, it should, in theory, have provided reasonable performance with better fuel efficiency. The 1974 GTO, available as an option on both the Ventura and Ventura Custom in two-door or hatchback forms, was more than just a badge and paint job. It was fitted with its own 350-cu in (5.735-liter) V8, which had actually been around since 1968, but there were some detail changes to suit this latest application. With a Quadrajet carburetor and mild cam timing, it produced 200 hp (149 kW) at 4,400 rpm. This was not in the 400-cu in class, but it did have that vibrating air scoop bulging out of the hood. The rest of the car betrayed its economy origins, with the bland bar speedometer only slightly offset by a little engine-turned appliqué, a reference to the 1964 original. Performance-wise, the Ventura GTO did not live up to its promise of a good performance/economy balance: road tests indicated a standing quarter mile in around 16 seconds, but only 12 mpg (5.5 liter/km). Still, some people liked it, and just over 7,000 GTOs were sold in 1974, a great improvement on the LeMans-based car of the previous year. It was not enough for Pontiac though, and the Ventura GTO experiment was not repeated in 1975.

A drag racing GTO from the early 1970s.

In 2004, the Pontiac GTO was relaunched in the U.S. market in the form of a rebadged, third-generation Holden Monaro.

It did not take long for hot-car fanatics to realize that a 400 or 455 V8 could be slotted straight into the Ventura/GTO, to the point where original 350s are now hard to find. This equals a smallish car plus a biggish engine, and that is where we came in.

The Pontiac GTO was relaunched in the United States in 2004, based on the Holden Monaro's V platform.

GM had high expectations to sell 18,000 units, but the Monaro-based GTO received a lukewarm reception in the U.S. The styling was frequently derided by critics as being too "conservative" and "anonymous" to befit either the GTO heritage or the current car's performance. In addition, the GTO faithful felt further insulted by GM's failure to present a U.S.-built car that incorporated any design lineage from the muscular icons of the 1960s and 1970s. Given the newly revived muscle car climate, it was also overshadowed by the Chrysler 300, the Dodge Charger, the Dodge Magnum, and the new Ford Mustang, which all featured more traditional "muscle" aesthetics. Sales were also limited because of dealer tactics, such as initially charging large markups and denying requests for test drives of the vehicle. By the end of the year, the 2004 vehicles were selling with significant discounts. Sales were 13,569 of 15,728 cars for 2004.

There were more modifications in 2005, but the car ceased production in 2006, marking the end of GTO's history.

A 2006 GTO with a nod to The Judge.

TEXT- DEPENDENT QUESTIONS

1. Name three people who influenced the creation of the GTO.

2. Name one important American automotive magazine.

3. Why did the popularity of muscle cars decline in the 1970s?

RESEARCH PROJECT

Write a report explaining why the Pontiac GTO is the most important muscle car of all time.

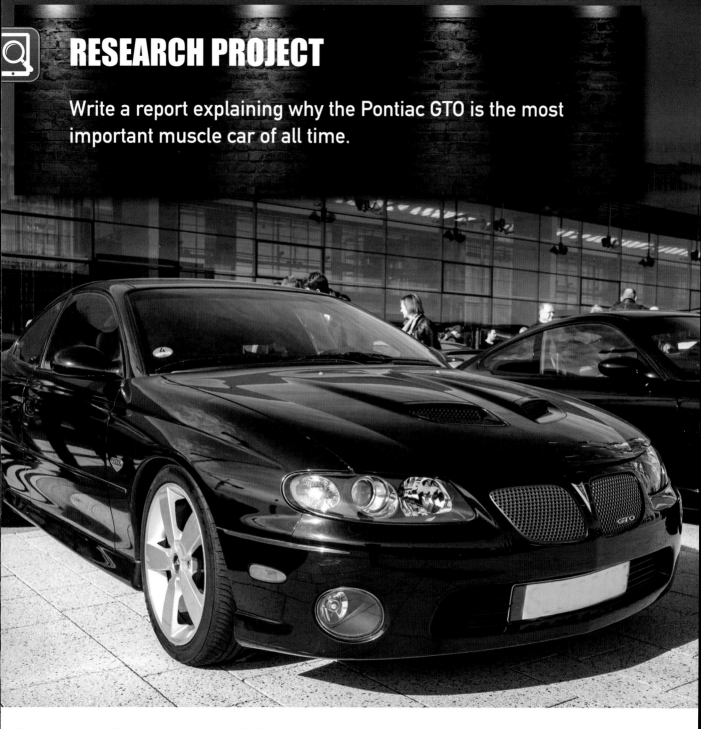

Production of the fifth-generation ended in 2006.

Pontiac GTO **73**

SERIES GLOSSARY OF KEY TERMS

acceleration	The process of moving faster or an increase in velocity.
aerodynamic	How efficiently an object is able to move through the air.
air scoop	An air inlet on the outer surface of automobile use to maintain a flow of air to a power plant or a ventilating system.
bodyshell	The outer casing of an automobile body, excluding doors, window glass, other fittings, and components.
camshaft	A shaft to which a cam is joined.
carburetor	A piece of apparatus for premixing vaporized fuel and air and supplying the mixture to an automobile's engine.
cylinder head	The closed end of a pump cylinder or automobile engine.
concept car	An automobile built to present a new design or technology.
crankshaft	A metal structure that connects an automobile's engine to the wheels enabling them to turn.
coupe	A two-door automobile, usually designed for two persons.
disc brakes	A brake operated by disc surfaces that rub together in the form of discs.
drag race	A competition in which drivers race vehicles at high speeds over a short, specified distance.
emissions	Substances discharged into the air by an automobile engine.
fastback	An automobile with a long, curving, and downward-sloping roof.
flagship	The most important one in a group—often used before another noun.
fuel injection	An electronically controlled system for injecting fuel into an automobile's engine.
gas-guzzler	An automobile that gets relatively poor mileage per gallon.
hardtop	An automobile with a permanent, rigid roof.
horsepower	A unit of power.
hot rod	An automobile rebuilt or modified for high speeds and power.
muscle car	Any of a group of American-made automobiles with powerful engines designed for high-performance driving.
NASCAR	National Association for Stock Car Auto Racing.
performance car	A sports car.
pickup truck	A light truck with an enclosed cab and an open body with low sides and tailgate.
piston	An engine part that slides back and forth inside a larger cylinder.
pony car	A type of two-door hardtop car with sporty styling and high performance.
production line	A line of machines operated by workers in a factory.
rear spoiler	An air deflector placed on the rear of an automobile to reduce lift at high speeds.
sedan	A two- or four-door automobile seating four or more persons and usually with an enclosed roof.
shock absorber	A device for absorbing the energy of sudden impulses or shocks in an automobile.
suspension	A system of springs supporting the upper part of an automobile on the axles.
tachometer	A device that measures how speed or velocity.
turbocharge	To supercharge an automobile's engine by means of a turbine-driven compressor.
torque	A force that produces or tends to produce rotation or torsion.
vehicle warranty	A promise by a manufacturer or dealer that it will repair or replace defects in an automobile for a specified period of time.

FURTHER READING

Bonaskiewich, David. *The Definitive Pontiac GTO Guide: 1964-1967*. Forest Lake, MN: Car Tech Inc. 2018.

Glastonbury, Jim. *Muscle Cars: Style, Power, and Performance*. Minneapolis, MN. Quarto Publishing Group, 2017.

Glatch, Tom. *The Complete Book of American Supercars*. Minneapolis, MN. Quarto Publishing Group, 2016.

Glatch, Tom and Lutz, Bob. *The Complete Book of Pontiac GTO: Every Model Since1964*. Minneapolis, MN. Quarto Publishing Group, 2018.

Holmstrom, Darwin. *GTO: Pontiac's Great One*. Minneapolis, MN. Crestline Books, 2018.

INTERNET RESOURCES

https://www.caranddriver.com *Car and Driver* is an American automotive enthusiast magazine. Its website offers interesting articles about the world of automobiles.

https://www.autotrader.com *Auto Trader* is an American website used for selling, valuing, and reviewing cars.

https://www.gm.com *General Motors* is a world-famous American car manufacturer. Its website provides useful information about the cars they produce.

https://www.britannica.com/topic/Ford-Motor-Company A useful resource into the history of the *Ford Motor Company*.

https://www.gentlemansgazette.com/muscle-cars-explained-history A useful website explaining the history of the muscle car and also some of the great models.

INDEX

AUTHOR'S BIOGRAPHY

Nicholas Tomkins is a full-time journalist and photographer specializing in writing articles about classic cars and motorcycles. His work was first published over ten years ago when he worked at a publishing house in London. Following his early career, he then went to live in New York for another leading publishing company, where he contributed to hundreds of books, magazines, and television programs. Additionally, Tomkins is an expert in the restoration of muscle cars of the 1960s and 1970s. To his credit, he has painstakingly restored at least four iconic cars to their former glory. Not just satisfied with his own hobby, Tomkins hosts workshops and training days for other would-be classic car restorers. Today, Tomkins lives and works near Exeter, England, where he works from home. He is married with two children.

PICTURE & VIDEO CREDITS